D0835359

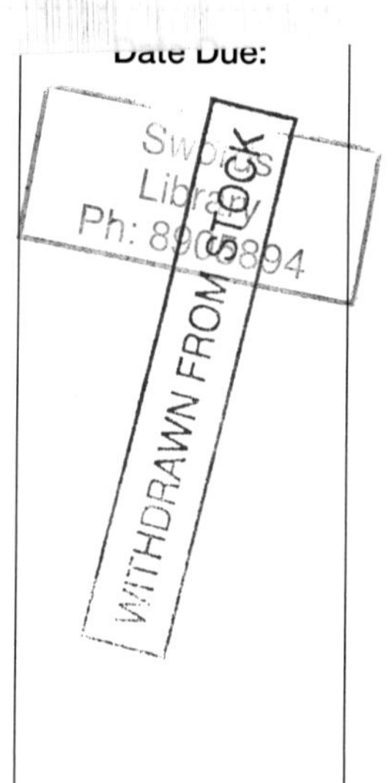
Swords
Library
Ph: 8905894
WITHDRAWN FROM STOCK

The A to Z of an Irish Christmas

All the Craic of the Crimbo!

Sarah Cassidy & Kunak McGann

First published 2020 by
The O'Brien Press Ltd,
12 Terenure Road East, Rathgar,
Dublin 6, D06 HD27, Ireland.
Tel: +353 1 4923333; Fax: +353 1 4922777
E-mail: books@obrien.ie; website: www.obrien.ie.
The O'Brien Press is a member of Publishing Ireland.

ISBN: 978-1-78849-213-3

Cover designed by Emma Byrne.

1 3 5 7 8 6 4 2
20 22 24 23 21

Printed and bound by Gutenberg Press, Malta.
The paper in this book is produced using pulp from managed forests.

Published in

THE A to Z OF AN IRISH CHRISTMAS

ALL THE CRAIC OF THE CRIMBO!

SARAH CASSIDY & KUNAK MCGANN

THE O'BRIEN PRESS
DUBLIN

airport arrivals

/eyr-port a-ryv-ulz/

noun. teary homecoming scenes

There is something so magical about the arrivals halls of the airports around our country in the run-up to Christmas. Family and friends are reunited from places near and far, often with babies and children in tow meeting their grandparents, aunties and uncles for the first time. Whatever you do, don't forget your hanky!

Andrews liver salts

/an-drooz liv-ur sawltz/

proper noun. aperitif

Back in the day, parents used to give their kids a pre-emptive glass of Andrews liver salts on Christmas morning in a bid to prevent the inevitable stomach aches from the rich food and sweets they were so unused to eating. The practice waned during the eighties, when

E numbers became a staple of the Irish diet and our stomachs evolved to handle anything.

annuals

/an-ew-ulz/
noun pl. rose-tinted reading

Beano, *Bunty*, *Dandy*, *Mandy & Judy*, *Shoot!*, *Twinkle*, *Victor* … Christmas wouldn't be Christmas without one of these hardback annuals wedged in your stocking. The perfect trip down memory lane – even Grandad can't resist a sneaky read of 'The Four Marys'.

Arnotts Santa

/ar-nutz san-ta/
proper noun. department store gift-giver

A tradition for many families is a trip to the capital city to look at the lights and visit Santa Claus. Every family has their favourite spot – from Switzer's and Clerys in days gone by, to St Stephen's Green and Arnotts, which are still going strong. Rumour has it the Arnotts guy is the real deal!

Away in a Manger

/a-wey in a meyn-jur/
song. mini-pops carol

Is there anything cuter than the sound of a school full of tea towel-clad children singing their little hearts out to 'Away in a Manger'? Watch out for those high notes!

B

Baileys

/bey-leez/

proper noun. heaven in a glass

The perfect accompaniment to EVERYTHING during the festive period! Elevates porridge from your humdrum midweek breakfast to a bowl of creamy goodness perfect for kickstarting your Christmas morning. Add a dash to your coffee, a drop over the pudding, or even a swirl in the cream to accompany a few mince pies while you drift in and out of consciousness by the fire and let the dinner digest.

Barry's Tea ad

/bar-eez tee ad/

proper noun. trip down memory lane

An ad that stops everyone in their tracks, this tale of a Dad buying a train set for his kids will warm even the coldest of hearts. Heard annually on the radio since 1994 and voiced by the late Peter Caffrey, it features the immortal line: 'Santa will bring them what they want, I said. This one's from me.' Awwww.

batteries

/bat-ur-eez/

noun pl. vital energy

In the busy run-up to Christmas, for God's sake don't forget to stock up on the batteries. Santa can't remember everything, you know. And hell hath no fury like a disappointed toddler.

The Big Clean-up

/thuh big kleen-up/
proper noun. determined dusting

The level and intensity of the pre-Christmas clean up usually depends on who is coming home. If someone is returning from Australia, Canada or Dubai with a new partner in tow, work will usually start in earnest at the beginning of December. Furniture is pulled out ('Did you see the amount of dust behind the washing machine?!'), curtains are whipped down, washed and dried, light fittings dusted and the good towels brought to the front of the hot press. If returning to your hometown from Dublin though, you'll be lucky if your bed is made.

The Big Fry

/thuh big fry/
proper noun. 'tis the season to be carefree

If you grill your sausages and bacon for the other fifty-one weeks of the year, caution is thrown to the wind on Christmas morning as your pork-based products are lashed in a pan, coated in glistening oil or butter (or both – sure it's Christmas!) and fried into crispy deliciousness. Bacon, sausages, pudding (black and white), potato cakes, mushrooms, tomatoes and eggs. Butter is slathered on thick slices of batch bread (Will I fry the bread? Sure, why not – the pan is hot!). All washed down with a steaming pot of tea, a glass of orange juice and a Baileys.

The Big Shop

/thuh big shop/
proper noun. mammoth stock-up

Probably the most important trip to the shops you will make in any given year. Involves precision timing: you don't want to hit the shops too early – no alcohol sales before 10.30am and a Christmas shop without alcohol just isn't a Christmas shop. But don't arrive too late either, or you'll be playing trolley wars as you make your way around EVERY aisle of a packed supermarket. Potatoes, Brussels sprouts, tins of chocolates, boxes of chocolates, tubs of chocolate, cheese, crackers, crisps … load that trolley up! And breadcrumbs – don't forget the breadcrumbs – and the cloves and the quince and the bumper box of Tayto and the tray of minerals. And the makings of a fry, or there'll be ructions.

Black Friday

/blak fry-dey/

event. consumerism of epic proportions

A new tradition in Ireland, Black Friday is the day after Thanksgiving in the States, when shops slash their prices in a bid to get people spending. In the last few years, it has taken off in Ireland and the UK, with shops and online retailers offering bargains on everything from electrical goods to clothing and even food. Next thing you know, we'll be waving the star-spangled banner on Independence Day.

board games

/bohrd geymz/

noun pl. fight!

The perfect end to a perfect day as the family gathers around after over-indulging at dinner and snoozing by the fire. Every family has their favourite – Monopoly, Pictionary, Taboo, 30 Seconds or Trivial Pursuit. The common denominator: no family can finish a game without somebody storming off, flinging the dice across the room or screaming 'It's not fair – they shouldn't be on the same team!' Such fun!

box of crisps

/boks uv krispz/

noun. potatoey goodness

No modern Irish Christmas is complete without a ridiculously over-sized cardboard box of crisps – a good old six-pack just won't do. Sure, they're so versatile: the perfect accompaniment to a turkey sandwich, and an ideal evening snack – simply serve between two slices of thick, buttered bread. King or Tayto? Family feuds have begun over less ...

bread sauce

/bred sawz/
noun. carb-loading

A delicious, thick, creamy sauce made from – you guessed it – bread. This sauce is the perfect accompaniment to the Christmas dinner because, you know, there may not be enough carbs in the ten types of potatoes being served.

bringing home the Christmas

/bring-ing hohm thuh kris-muss/
phrase. hunter-gathering

Back in the days before Credit Union loans, there was a tradition that people would travel to the nearest town in the run-up to Christmas to sell their own produce: butter, eggs, poultry and vegetables. Any money made was spent on toys and food for the family, so they came home literally 'bringing the Christmas' with them – making them as welcome as Santy himself!

Brown Thomas window

/brown tom-iss win-doh/
proper noun. upmarket display

Every year, crowds gather around the windows of Brown Thomas in Dublin, Cork, Limerick and Galway, to gawk at their marvellous window displays. Always beautiful, extravagant and over the top, filled with designer clothes, handbags and – let's face it – products that are way out of most of our price ranges. But hey, it's free to look and we can always dream!

Brussels sprouts

/bruh-sulz sprowtz/
noun pl. mini-cabbages

Sprouts with your dinner? It's the age-old question that splits the Irish population down the middle. And now science has explained why. About half of us have a mutated gene that leaves us immune to a bitter-tasting chemical found in sprouts. Without that mutation, nothing will entice you to eat those suckers. Not even if they're fried with bacon.

busking

/bus-king/
verb. free open-air concert

You can't call yourself an Irish singer-songwriter if you haven't joined the ranks of performers who have busked around Grafton Street on Christmas Eve. Bono, Imelda May, Hozier, Glen Hansard and Liam Ó Maonlaí, to name but a few, have all given up their time to raise money for the homeless in this most gorgeous and generous of Irish Christmas traditions.

C

candle in the window

/kan-dul in thuh win-dow/
tradition. hazardous guide home

One of Ireland's oldest traditions is to place a candle in the window on Christmas Eve as a sign of welcome to all. Traditionally, the youngest member of the family would light the candle, but nowadays they're often battery operated – nobody wants to bother the poor fire brigade on Christmas Eve.

cards

/kardz/
noun pl. festive post

The world is made up of two types of people: those who send Christmas cards and those who don't. But whichever camp you're in, a sturdy white envelope with a cheery Christmas stamp on it makes a welcome change from the usual bills and circulars. Thank you, postie!

carols

/ka-rulz/

noun pl. Christmas tunes

From religious songs such as 'Silent Night', 'Away in a Manger' and 'Little Donkey', 'The Holly and the Ivy', 'O Come All Ye Faithful' and 'Good King Wenceslas' to secular classics like 'Jingle Bells' and 'Rudolph the Red-nosed Reindeer' – the list of Christmas carols is endless, and everyone has their favourite. Whether you've the voice of an angel or haven't a note in your head – sing them loud and sing them proud!

chairs

/cheyrz/

noun pl. seating plan

The dining room table in most family homes is made to sit about four to six people. So the extended family Christmas dinner means chairs and stools of all differing heights and sizes being drafted in from wherever possible. Or you can always repurpose other household items. Think: the good nest of tables, the upturned coal bucket, or the kitchen bin.

Cheeky Charlies

/chee-kee char-leez/

noun pl. treats for the chisellers

'Get the last of your Cheeky Charlies!' A famous refrain from Dublin traders who sold everything from toy monkeys to sheets of wrapping paper – 'Five for fifty!' What a bargain.

cheeseboard

/cheez-bohrd/
noun. lactose-loading

The perfect antidote to Monopoly-induced family rows, the cheese board is usually brought out late on Christmas night (but not too late – who wants Christmas-themed nightmares?!). Cheddar, brie, gouda, blue and goat's cheese, accompanied by honey, grapes, chutney … maybe some quince if you're feeling fancy, and a big box of crackers. Just when you thought you couldn't possibly eat another bite. Best served with a glass or two of port.

Christmas Day outfit

/kris-muss dey owt-fit/
noun. the good clothes

Traditionally on Christmas morning, out came the new clothes (red or tartan for that extra festive touch), the nicely-polished shoes and the spotless coat. All over the country, children looked their very best. For the first half hour at least.

Christmas Day swim

/kris-muss dey swim/

event. goosebump-inducing mania

Christmas morning will see hordes of people taking a dip in the chilly sea at beaches up and down the country. The cold shock and exercise is great for parents trying to shake off the tiredness of the 4am wake-up, and clears a hangover better than a box of paracetamol and a large coffee.

Christmas Eve

/kris-muss eev/

event. the night before Christmas

The second most wonderful day of the year. The air is thick with anticipation: Santa is on the way, presents are wrapped, the ham is boiled, the vegetables are prepped. And if you don't have kids, it's off to the local for a Christmas tipple or three …

Christmas FM

/kris-muss eff-em/

proper noun. non-stop seasonal tunes

Since its beginnings in 2008, Christmas FM has become a key part of the run-up to Christmas in Ireland. A radio station that plays festive tunes all day, every day, while raising money for charity – it's like a perennial Band Aid.

Christmas No. 1

/kris-muss num-ber wun/

proper noun. top of the pops

Back when 'Top of the Pops' was unmissable and you had to actually go to a shop to buy music, the Christmas No. 1 was a big deal. The accolade has been won by some of the biggest acts on the planet, from Take That to The Beatles and Whitney Houston, and not forgetting Mr Blobby, Bob the Builder and our very own Zig and Zag! While the Spice Girls topped the charts the world over with '2 become 1', us Irish felt it was more fitting that Dustin the Turkey's rendition of 'Rat Trap' come in at No. 1. Everyone loves a good turkey at Christmas.

The Christmas Party

/thuh kris-muss par-tee/
event. annual knees-up

The one night of the year when employees get to tell their boss exactly how they feel as they strut their stuff on the dancefloor. There's nothing quite like scrolling through jobs.ie while nursing the hangover from hell.

Christmas pyjamas

/kris-muss puh-jah-maz/
noun. novelty nightwear

Christmas pyjamas are the new good clothes for Christmas. Fleece, cotton, satin, a onesie or a two piece – there are options to suit everyone and anyone. A glance through Instagram on Christmas Eve will reveal a worrying trend though: entire families in matching pyjamas … *shudder*

coal from Santy

/kohl frum san-tee/
noun. empty parental threat

Every. Child's. Nightmare.

cranberry sauce

/cran-bur-ee sawss/
noun. Christmas jam

Bought to accompany the Christmas turkey. Usually languishes at the back of the fridge before being thrown out in July.

crib

/krib/

noun. baby Jesus's gaff

Part of the Christmas decorations, a crib can be found in many Irish homes. Depicting the scene of Jesus's birth, it contains figures of Mary, Joseph and the three wise men – and a few farm animals usually make an appearance. And the baby Jesus, of course. Technically he shouldn't appear until Christmas Day, but better to put him in as soon as the rest of the decorations go up, or he might be forgotten. And it literally wouldn't be Christmas without Jesus!

D

December 8th

/kris-mus shop-ing dey/

event. Irish Black Friday

Back before shopping centres existed on the outskirts of almost every Irish town, people used to travel in their droves up to Dublin city for Christmas shopping. December 8th was a holy day and schools used to close so that everyone could attend mass. Instead they shopped till they dropped.

The Dinner

/thuh din-ur/

event. a mountain of a meal

Talked about for weeks beforehand, the preparation for this meal is almost as important as the meal itself.

How many are you cooking for? How big is your bird? Do you boil the ham the night before? What do you mean, your turkey's not organic?! Turkey, goose, baked ham, spiced beef, sausage stuffing, bread stuffing, duck fat roast potatoes, potato croquettes, garlic potatoes, mash, Brussels sprouts, carrots, turnips, peas, cabbage, gravy, bread sauce, cranberry sauce. Pile it high. Then sleep it off.

duck fat

/duk fat/

noun. extra fatty roasting oil

For some reason, at Christmas it is imperative that the potatoes are roasted in delicious, calorific duck fat – not even the good, organic olive oil your aunt Geraldine pressed with her bare feet in Italy will suffice. We blame Nevin Maguire.

Dustin the turkey

/dust-in thuh turk-ee/

proper noun. poultry puppet

This turkey vulture first appeared on Irish television screens in 1989, as part of 'The Den' with Zig and Zag. He was to be fattened up and eaten for Christmas dinner, but managed to avoid his fate by winning a place in everyone's hearts. He has since performed at the Eurovision and sung with the likes of Bob Geldof, Boyzone, Joe Dolan and Ronnie Drew. What a ledge!

E

early start

/ur-lee start/

noun. Christmas morning with the kids

With excitement building all year, it's no wonder that the kids aren't going to sleep in on Christmas morning. Most parents are lucky if they make it past 6am, and then stumble around, bleary-eyed, trying to work up enthusiasm for the incredibly loud toys that have just been gifted. Spare a thought for those poor unfortunates whose kids woke up *right after* Santa made his delivery. God bless them, every one.

Elf

/elf/

film. modern classic

Released in 2003, the story of Buddy the Elf can be quoted by most humans with a television. A Christmas classic for a reason. Don't be a cotton-headed ninny muggins – give it a watch.

F

Fairytale of New York

/feyr-ee-tayl uv nyoo yawrk/

song. controversial carol

Sung by Shane McGowan and Kirsty McColl, 'Fairytale of New York' has been voted Ireland's favourite Christmas song of all time. Move over Mariah, Noddy and Shakin' Stevens, there is no other song that unites a crowd in a bar at Christmas time like this one can. Altogether now: 'And the boys from the NYPD choir were singing "Galway Bay", and the bells were ringing out for Christmas Day!'

family row

/fam-il-ee row/

noun. Christmas tradition

Spending hours on end trapped indoors with your family, overtired from an early start with the kids and possibly feeling a little the worse for wear are the ideal conditions to start a family row. It can be over anything – from not wanting to watch *The Snowman* again to somebody leaving the cream off the shopping list, but there's a good chance it's because someone forgot to remind Santa Claus to buy batteries or robbed all the money from the Monopoly bank. Merry Christmas one and all!

feeding the cake

/fee-ding thuh keyk/

verb. alcoholic inflation

No, Granny is not sneaking into the wardrobe to have a snifter of whiskey, she is feeding the cake! To have the most deliciously moist cake, it is necessary to give it an auld tipple every couple of weeks before covering it in a thick layer of icing. Whiskey, brandy or rum usually does the job; the cake's not picky.

Forty Foot

/for-tee fut/

place. diving into the festive season

Probably the most famous Christmas Day swim in the country, the Forty Foot makes for great pictures on the front pages. Immortalised in James Joyce's *Ulysses*, this legendary bathing spot on the southern tip of Dublin Bay is the perfect spot for a quick dive before Christmas dinner. Bracing!

Funderland

/fun-dur-land/

proper noun. the musies

Nothing helps shake off the cabin fever that can set in over Christmas like a trip to Funderland at the RDS. Europe's largest indoor amusement park has it all – a massive Ferris wheel, waltzers, bumper cars and even a circus and ice-skating rink. You might need a credit union loan to get you through the day, but isn't it worth it for a day out of the house?

G

gifts

/gifts/

noun pl. damned if you do, damned if you don't

Christmas present-buying can be a minefield: who to buy for, how much to spend, is it really okay to give socks? Some people are mega-prepared, picking up a present a month throughout the year and announcing smugly in November that they're 'all set'. The rest of us scramble around in December, desperately trying to make the right choices, muttering under our breath that 'It's the thought that counts'. Until you get a hoover from your partner, that is.

goose

/gooss/

noun. alternative bird

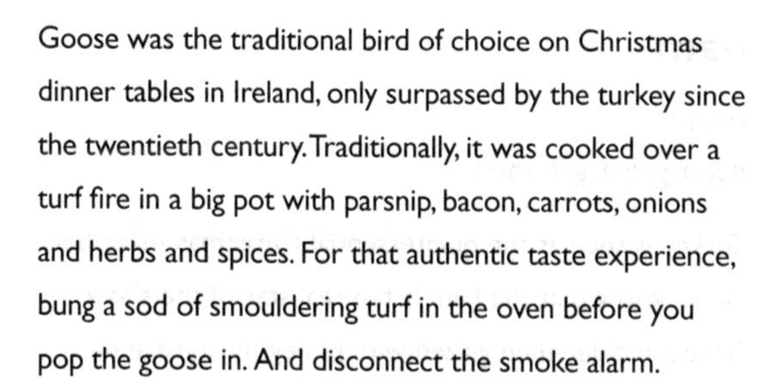

Goose was the traditional bird of choice on Christmas dinner tables in Ireland, only surpassed by the turkey since the twentieth century. Traditionally, it was cooked over a turf fire in a big pot with parsnip, bacon, carrots, onions and herbs and spices. For that authentic taste experience, bung a sod of smouldering turf in the oven before you pop the goose in. And disconnect the smoke alarm.

Guinness ad

/gin-iss ad/

proper noun. top tv

If ever there was an ad to give you all the feels it's the Guinness Christmas ad. First aired in 2014, it combines evocative scenes of Christmas Eve, the beauty of Ireland blanketed in fresh snow, and that voiceover: 'Even at the home of the black stuff, they dream of a white one.' Iconic!

Irish tearjerkers

/ay-rish teer-jur-kurz/
noun pl. watch 'em and weep

My Left Foot, Philomena, Song for a Raggy Boy, Angela's Ashes … If there's a film about a miserable Irish childhood, you'll find it on the RTÉ Christmas schedule.

It's a Wonderful Life

/itz uh wun-dur-ful lyf
film. restore your faith in humanity

Directed by Frank Capra and starring James Stewart and Donna Reed, this film was deemed too depressing for the holiday season on its release in 1946. Fast forward and it is now considered one of the best films of all time, and required viewing every December. Whose heart doesn't melt when they hear that line 'Every time a bell rings, an angel gets his wings'?

It's Chriiiiiiiiistmas!

/itz kriiiiiiiiiiis-mus/

phrase. festive announcement

Noddy Holder's unadulterated cheer towards the end of Slade's 1973 classic 'Merry Xmas Everybody', which sold over a million copies and stormed to the top of the charts. It heralds the beginning of full-on, devil-may-care Christmas. Bring it on.

J

James Joyce

/jey-umz joys/

proper noun. literary genius

Ireland's answer to *A Christmas Carol*, James Joyce's 'The Dead', the final short story from *Dubliners*, is one of his most enduring and accessible works. Apparently the Americans believe that we sit around and read the story together on Christmas Eve. I'm sure some of us do …

January sales

/djan-yoo-eyree seylz/

event. new year madness

Great time to buy the decorations for next Christmas. And soap sets. Lots of soap sets.

jokes

/johkz/

noun pl. cracker-fillers

Who hides in a bakery at Christmas?

A mince spy.

What do you get if you eat Christmas decorations?

Tinselitis.

What did Adam say the day before Christmas?

It's Christmas, Eve.

jumpers

/jum-purz/

noun pl. seasonal geansaí

Ireland just cannot get enough of Christmas jumpers. And these days, there is such a range of patterns to choose from. Will you go for an old favourite like a brightly coloured Christmas tree, reindeer, Santa or snowman? Or change it up a bit with added tinsel or flashing lights? You could even opt for one that plays

'Jingle Bells' when someone brushes past you.

And who doesn't love the person who arrives to the party with their ever-witty 'I'm on the naughty list' or 'Do my baubles look big in this?' jumper? Baubles. *snigger*

K

Kids' movies

/kidz moo-veez/

noun pl. yuletide viewing

Nothing puts you in a Christmas mood quite like seeing those movie classics hitting the TV screens in December: *Home Alone, Elf, Charlie and the Chocolate Factory, The Sound of Music, Mary Poppins* and *Chitty Chitty Bang Bang.* An essential part of any childhood Christmas.

Kris Kindle

/kris kin-dul/

proper noun. Secret Santa

Your mission should you choose to accept it: buy a uniquely meaningful, beautiful or amusing present for Ciara in accounts, who you've spoken to once and were convinced was actually called Catherine. Spend no more than €10. Then have Ciara open said present in front of everyone you both work with. There's no way this ends well.

L

last-minute shopping

/last min-ut shop-ing/

noun. playing it cool

There are some people that start making Christmas-present lists in January, often using complicated Excel spreadsheets, carefully planning those special gifts that will make each of their loved ones light up with happiness. And then there are those who manage to hoover up the gifts they need in a frantic half hour just before the shops close on Christmas Eve. You all know who you are.

The Late Late Toy Show

/thuh leyt leyt toi shoh/

TV prog. it's beginning to look a lot like …

A Christmas jumper-clad host, the latest toys and gadgets reviewed by adorably precocious kids, heart-warming musical performances and tear-jerking moments. An institution.

Lemon's Season's Greetings

/leh-munz see-zunz gree-tingz/

proper noun. sugary assortment

Lemon's sweets have been an Irish staple since the mid-1800s, even scoring a mention in James Joyce's *Ulysses.* Their bestselling assortment has always been Season's Greetings, which is brim-full of everything from liquorice toffees to chocolate fudge, buttery caramels to fruit jellies. Just clapping eyes on that smiling Santa on the front of the box is enough to lift your Christmas spirit.

letter to Santy

/leh-tur too san-tee/
noun. message for the man

Nowadays, there are a few different options for getting your letter to the North Pole – as well as the traditional method of whooshing it up the chimney, you can let An Post take care of it, or even pop it into the dedicated post box in your local supermarket. Regardless of how it gets there, never forget that, to a child, it's the most important letter they will ever write. No changing your mind after it's sent!

lights

/lytz/
noun pl. bright ideas

A generation ago, those who put a set of lights in their porch were just showing off. Nowadays, Christmas lights have become an extreme sport. It's not just lights strung in the branches of the tree in the front garden – there are giant flashing mangers, luminous life-size Santas, and snowflakes and reindeer projected onto the front of the house. Stuck for something to do with the kids during the holidays? Wait till dusk and take a drive around the local estates – and prepare for the oohs and aahs from the back seat.

M

midnight mass

/mid-nyt mas/

event. nocturnal religious service

The annual Christmas Eve outing, in which prodigal sons and daughters join their parents in the pews for a blessing. Nowadays it starts at 9pm, to minimise the attendance of the inebriated, or at least to delay the inebriation just a little.

mince pies

/mins pyz/

noun pl. deceptively named sweet treats

Popular hundreds of years ago, traditional mince pies were a way of preserving meat by adding suet and spices. In more modern times, they've become meat-free, rounder and sweeter, and are the perfect accompaniment to a cup of tea when those Christmas visitors pop over. At their very best served fresh-from-the-oven warm with a dollop of whiskey cream.

mistletoe

/mis-ul-toh/

noun. frisky flora

The favourite winter plant of romantics everywhere, you'll recognise mistletoe by its pairs of oval, evergreen leaves and clusters of white berries. Ancient Celts believed that mistletoe had strong healing powers, causing it to be banned by the powers-that-be. Now banned by nervous HR departments everywhere in the run-up to the office Christmas party.

moving crib

/moo-ving krib/
noun. model manger

Dublin's moving crib in Parnell Square uses mechanical figures to bring the story of the Nativity to life. On the go for over sixty years, parents and even grandparents who visited the crib as children are keeping the tradition alive by bringing their own families to this popular festive attraction. Pop in and see Bethlehem in the rare auld times.

mulled wine

/muld wyn/
noun. timely beverage

If the Christmas spirit and general feeling of good will towards all aren't enough to give you a warm glow, then something a little stronger is called for. That's where mulled wine comes in. Gently warm some red wine, add cloves, oranges, sugar and spices, and hey presto – liquid refreshment that is guaranteed to insulate you against the cold weather and bring a flush to your cheeks. Combine with mince pies for maximum festive cheer.

must-have toy

/must-hav toy/

noun. Christmas quest

From Cabbage Patch Kids, Mr Frosty and the Big Yellow Teapot to Hatchimals, LOL dolls and Buzz Lightyear, every year there's that one toy that every kid wants and every parent will do anything to get their hands on. There's no telling what lengths they'll go to when they spot the last one on a shelf. Nothing says Christmas like a brawl in the aisle of Smyths Toys.

N

Nativity

/neh-tiv-it-ee/

event. child stars

For a few precious years, the annual Nativity play is the chance to coo over your talented little darling as they forget the words of 'Little Donkey' or announce that there's no room at the inn. Watch out for all the imaginative costuming on display – Joseph? One of the three kings? A shepherd? A dressing gown and a tea-towel on the head will do nicely.

New Year

/nyoo yeer/
event. out with the old

There are numerous Irish traditions around the New Year, including setting a place at New Year's dinner for those who have passed away during the year, and forecasting good luck if the first person through the front door has black hair. And let's not forget the custom of banging on the doors and walls with bread – yes, bread – to chase bad luck from the family home. A uniquely fun way to ring in the New Year.

Nollaig Shona Duit

/nul-ug hun-a dich/
Irish phrase. Happy Christmas

After fourteen years of learning the Irish language, you can absolutely bank on people knowing two phrases: 'An bhfuil cead agam dul go dtí an leithreas?' and 'Nollaig Shona Duit'. Hard to imagine getting through life without either of those.

not getting dressed

/not geh-ting dresd/
verb. staying in pyjamas

Yes, it's okay. Really. With the luxury of a few days off around Christmas, it's time to put those new festive pyjamas, slippers and fluffy socks to good use.

novelty gifts

/nov-ul-tee giftz/
noun pl. cheeky tat

The Santa hat. The elf ears. The musical tie. The antler hairclips. The pudding specs. Christmas doesn't get more hilarious than this.

O

over-indulgence

/oh-vur in-dul-juns/

noun. just one more

Moderation in everything, including moderation. The diet can wait till the New Year.

orange

/or-unj/

noun. the original stocking-filler

Hailing from a time when the gift of a piece of fruit was a really big deal, the tradition of putting oranges in stockings has been around for donkey's years. Whether it's a mandarin, clementine or satsuma (and does anyone know the difference anyway?), that little bit of vitamin C is a great boost for the immune system during the demanding festive season. And if you're lucky, it might even come with a chocolate coin or two.

P

panto

/pan-toh/

noun. fairytale fun

Sold out from November to mid-January, the traditional panto is jam-packed with flamboyant costumes, cheeky jokes and anyone from A- to Z-list celebrities. The main male lead is played by a woman, the Dame is played by a man, and the horse is played by two people. It's a hoot. Thinking of giving it a miss this year? Oh no, you're not!

poc fada

/puk faw-dah/

event. proof of hurling prowess

The poc fada ('long puck') involves pucking a sliotar with a hurley around a 5km course. It was first undertaken in the Cooley Mountains, in remembrance of the mighty Setanta who, as everyone knows, was a great man for the hurling. Has become a traditional event for many parishes over the festive season, often for a worthy local cause. Winning it secures you bragging rights for a whole year.

posting dates

/poh-sting deytz/

noun pl. final countdown

When An Post release their final Christmas posting dates for destinations worldwide, it's time to get cracking on those Irish care packages: Tayto for the cousin in Dubai, Cadbury's for the sister in Sydney, and tea bags for the uncle in Queens. There'll be tears if you don't get them to their destination before the zoom call on the 25th. The pressure.

pudding

/puh-ding/

noun. more dried fruit than you can shake a stick at

There is an art to making the perfect Christmas pud, and if you can't master it yourself, you should find a family member or neighbour who'll take your yearly order. Puddings are traditionally made on the Sunday before Advent, which leaves plenty of time for the spices to mellow and all that juicy fruit to plump up. Raisins, sultanas, currants, chopped cherries, mixed peel, and even a lemon, orange or apple – one serving of this and that's your five-a-day sorted.

Q

quality time

/kwal-i-tee tym/

noun. home for the Christmas

Most of us can't wait for all that quality family time at Christmas – catching up with the folks, having a laugh with the siblings, playing games with the kids. But never forget the golden rule: it's quality, not quantity. For the love of your sanity, don't overdo it.

queuing

/kyoo-ing/

verb. worth the wait

You know Christmas is coming when the amount of time you spend in queues goes up – queuing in cars to get into the shopping centre car park, queuing at tills in every shop, queuing with the kids for the Santa visit, queuing for pints at the bar. All while listening to 'Last Christmas' and 'All I Want for Christmas Is You' on a loop. Fun times.

R

races

/rey-suz/

event. at a gallop

Horse racing is one of Ireland's most popular sports, and there is nothing better than heading to the racetrack over the festive period to catch up with friends and get some fresh air. Go on, get your glad rags on and back a longshot!

raffles

/raf-ulz/

noun pl. if you're not in you can't win

Every parish, GAA club and community centre worth its salt has a Christmas raffle to raise funds. And you can report them for criminal negligence if the prizes don't include a turkey, a ham, a bottle of whiskey and a tin of USA biscuits.

re-gifting

/ree-gif-ting/

verb. present recycling

Whether it's a voucher, a candle or a tin of biscuits, the craze for zero waste has made it perfectly acceptable to pass on things that just aren't to your taste. Just be sure to follow these very important rules: (i) check the best-before date on any perishables; (ii) ALWAYS check for gift tags or inscriptions – nothing says 're-gift' like a book dedicated to you; and (iii) make sure you remember where the gift came from – re-gifting an item back around to its original giver is a cardinal sin.

reindeer

/reyn-deer/

noun pl. all the jingle ladies

Dasher, Dancer, Prancer, Vixen, Comet, Cupid, Donner, Blitzen – and don't forget Rudolph. Every child knows that Santa's team of reindeer are an integral part of the magic of Christmas, helping him deliver presents to all the girls and boys. For grown-ups, remembering all nine reindeer usually means a handy point in the Christmas quiz.

Roses

/roh-zus/

proper noun. contentious confectionery

Cadbury's Roses have been around since the 1930s, and were named after Rose Brothers, the company that supplied the machines that wrapped the chocolates. Nowadays, you can't walk into any self-respecting Irish home at Christmas without tripping over a tub. And you can tell a lot about a household from their favourite sweets. First to go should be the Hazel in Caramel, followed by the Golden Barrel or the Hazel Whirl. If you're with a family who leave till last anything but the strawberry, coffee or orange, get your coat and make your excuses.

RTÉ Guide

/ar-tee-ee gyd/
proper noun. what's on the telly?

Even in these days of content-on-demand, there's still something immensely satisfying about sitting down with the Christmas edition of the *RTÉ Guide* to mark up all the TV specials and films coming up over the holidays. Put on the kettle and grab that red pen – we're keeping it old school.

S

Santa Claus

/san-tah klawz/
proper noun. ho ho ho

Santa Claus, Santy, Daidí na Nollag, Father Christmas, Saint Nicholas, Kris Kringle, Jolly Old Elf, The Man in the Red Suit. Doesn't matter what you call him as long as you B-E-L-I-E-V-E.

Santa snack

/san-tah snak/
noun. midnight feast

A glass of milk and a saucer of rich tea? A pint of Guinness and a mince pie? A glass of whiskey and a slice of Christmas cake? It's all good – Santa loves a varied diet. And there's a reason he needs eight reindeer to pull his sleigh.

Santa watch

/san-tah wach/

noun. keeping tabs on the man in red

Back in the day, children could either listen to the big man himself in his annual radio interview or watch footage of him setting off from the North Pole on Christmas Eve's Six O'Clock News. Nowadays, Santa will email the kids personalised video messages, there are apps to record him arriving in your sitting room, and NORAD uses satellites to track his progress around the world. Welcome to the new millennium, Santa!

selection box

/seh-lek-shun boks/

noun. chocolatey deliciousness

Possibly the most fun a child can ever have is eating the entire contents of a selection box, then replacing the wrappers to make it look like it's still full. Sooo disappointing for the brother or sister looking forward to digging into it for Stephen's Day breakfast!

sing-song

/sing sawng/
noun. Christmas crooning

Let's face it, the Irish will use any opportunity for a sing-song, and Christmas and New Year are no exception. As well as the old reliables like 'The Wild Rover' and 'Danny Boy', expect a nod to the time of year with 'Fairytale of New York' and maybe even a verse of 'Do They Know It's Christmas?', with added Bono theatrics: 'Well tonight, thank God it's them instead of you!'

smoked salmon

/smohkd sa-mun/
noun. fishy first course

Even if you wouldn't touch a bit of smoked salmon from one end of the year to the other, it's bound to make an appearance as the Christmas Day starter. A slab of homemade brown bread slathered in butter and topped with a slice of smoked salmon, a dash of pepper and a squeeze of lemon juice. Add a few capers for those with notions. Then get on with the real work: The Dinner.

soaps

/sohpz/
noun pl. Christmas cliffhangers

One thing you can bank on with the soaps at Christmas is DRAMA. 'EastEnders' had Dirty Den serving Angie divorce papers up for dinner, 'Coronation Street' had Cilla Battersby blowing up the chippy, and 'Emmerdale' had THAT plane crash. Fair City had much smaller budgets.

spiced beef

/spysd beef/
noun. rebels' rump

A traditional Christmas treat in Cork, the beef is cured for at least three months in flavour-boosters such as stout, cider, juniper berries and pimento. The recipes are as varied as they are secret. They could tell you but then they'd have to kill you.

sponsored runs

/spon–surd runz/
event. jingle bell joggin'

From the Goal Mile to the Reindeer Dash and the Santa Run, there are lots of ways to get fit while raising money for charity during the festive period. And remember, the faster you run, the more mince pies you can eat. Now that's motivation!

Stephen's Day

/stee-vunz dey

event. the aftermath

Christmas Day is full of commitments – as well as the mammoth feat of making the dinner, there's mass, heading to Granny and Grandad's to show them the kids' presents, welcoming Uncle Martin in for a tipple before dinner, and having the neighbours over for a mince pie supper. So, if you can manage it, Stephen's Day should be all about the couch, the telly and the turkey sandwiches. Aaaaaaand relax.

Stephen's Day sales

/stee-vunz dey seylz/

event. endurance retail therapy

For those who don't fancy taking it easy on Stephen's Day, there is the madcap option of rolling out your sleeping bag and spending Christmas night camped outside the local shopping centre or department store in anticipation of the next morning's sales. Only to be considered by those who don't feel the cold, with world-class bladder control.

Stephen's Night

/stee-vunz nyt/

event. getting the old gang back together

Everyone is home for the few days and making their way to the old hangouts, it's the last night the DJ can get away with playing Slade and Wizzard, and people are dying to let loose after being cooped up with the family. And no work tomorrow. Stephen's Night has all the makings of an epic night out.

T

table

/tey-bul/

noun. dinner's ready!

For that one day in the year, your dinner table is all dressed up. Not just the freshly ironed linen tablecloth, but the antique lace runner and the special Christmas centrepiece, the wedding present silver cutlery, all polished up, and the glittering Waterford Crystal glasses. Sure, everyone loves a bit of fine dining.

too early

/too ur-lee/

phrase. it's not even Halloween yet

We've all done it: turned to someone and tut-tutted that Christmas is coming earlier and earlier every year.

When they open the Christmas sections of department stores in early September, or you see chocolate Santas on the shelves alongside chocolate pumpkins, or you hear your first Christmas song on the radio in November. There's build-up and then there's BUILD-UP.

tree

/tree/

noun. something to put the presents under

The great debate: real or artificial? Artificial trees are more convenient – just drag it down from the attic and assemble – but can anything make up for not having that divine pine tree smell wafting through the house? The pine needles on the floor, the scratches on the hall walls, and the time spent trying to squeeze it into the wheelie bin in January – all totally worth it.

trifle

/try-ful/

noun. dessert to die for

Flirt with those modern desserts if you like – the espresso ice-cream and the deconstructed lemon tart – but you'll go a long way before you find anything that'll beat the retro classic that is Mammy's trifle. Alternate layers of sherry-soaked sponge, custard and jelly or fresh fruit in a large bowl, top with cream, and sprinkle with flaked almonds. Then just hope against hope there's enough left for seconds.

turkey tray

/tur-kee trey/

noun. bird basting

Despite the fact that most houses have a perfectly good reusable roasting tray in a kitchen press, people feel the need to buy a large aluminium version as part of the Big Christmas Shop. It says 'turkey' on it so it's a necessity, right?

TV specials

/tee-vee spesh-ulz/
noun pl. festive watching

The perfect post-Christmas dinner TV viewing – a special version of your favourite TV show. From 'Father Ted' to 'Mrs Brown's Boys', 'Only Fools and Horses' to 'Gavin & Stacey', there's something for everyone. And if it's not quite your cup of tea, don't worry – you'll probably doze off in a few minutes anyway.

Twelve Pubs of Christmas

/twelv pubz uv kris-muss/
event. daredevil drinking

Gangs of people in Christmas jumpers, twelve pubs, twelve drinks, one night. Not for the faint-hearted.

U

unexpected present

/un-ex-pek-tud prez-unt/
noun. surprise surprise

When that neighbour from six doors up turns up with a beautifully wrapped present, and you don't have anything for her. Time for some emergency wrapping! Somebody grab that jar of bath salts that's been sitting in the ensuite since 2016.

USA biscuits

/yoo-ess-ey biz-kits/
proper noun. 100-year-old confectionery

A perennial favourite in Irish homes, USA biscuits were first produced over a hundred years ago and named when America joined World War I. There's not a mammy or daddy's favourite biscuit that's not included – from pink wafers to bourbons, jammy dodgers to custard creams. Just remember the most important rule of biscuit tin etiquette: NEVER start the second layer before the first is completely empty.

V

viral homecomings

/vy-rul hohm-cum-ingz/

noun pl. Mammy, I'm home!

A growing craze in recent years, returning sons and daughters have taken to filming their surprise homecomings and posting them online. Cue shrieks of joy, inappropriate language and many tears as the poor parents come to terms with the delighted shock of having their long-lost offspring home for the Christmas. Lump-in-the-throat viewing.

visit to Santa

/vi-zit too san-ta/

event. annual encounter

In the run-up to Christmas, there are Santies everywhere: from shopping centres and country houses to forest parks and pet farms. Once you're booked in somewhere (and booking is highly recommended), children's anticipation of meeting the man in red can send them into a tizzy of excitement. Once they're actually perched on his knee, with Santa asking them what they've put on their list, don't be surprised if this excitement manifests as muteness. Sure, it's all too much for them, poor things.

Women's Christmas

/wi-minz kris-mus/

proper noun. Little Christmas

Celebrated on the sixth of January, Women's Christmas is also known as Little Christmas or Nollaig na mBan. Traditionally, this was the day when, after toiling hard to feed everyone over the Christmas, women could finally down tools while the menfolk picked up the slack. Nowadays, you'd hope that a better division of labour makes Women's Christmas less a necessity and more of a timely reminder of the value and strength of Irish women. Girl power, Irish style.

wren boys

/ren boyz/

proper noun. penny for the wren

The wren has long been maligned as 'the Devil's bird' for giving away the hiding place of St Stephen and for betraying Irish soldiers who were setting up for an ambush. In many parts of Ireland, 26 December traditionally saw wrens being hunted, stuck on top of a pole and paraded from house to house – with people donating a penny 'to bury the wren'. Nowadays, wren boys (and girls!), also called mummers, dress up in old clothes – sometimes wearing straw hats or suits – and sing and play music, collecting money for local charities. *Disclaimer: no wrens are actually harmed during the celebration of this event.*

Ever wondered about the healing powers of dock leaves, flat 7UP and Sudocrem?

Confused about the difference between 'going out' and 'going out-out'?

Well, wonder no more. This handy A to Z is packed with insider knowledge and quirky Irishisms for locals and blow-ins alike. Read it or we'll tell your Mammy you left the immersion on!

'Don't mind me, I'm only your mother.'

World–renowned for her unique perspective on life, there is no-one quite like the Irish Mammy. From the weather t your choice of clothing the quintessential Irish Mam has something to say on every subject.

This handy collection of Mammyisms will ensure you are never without an Irish Mammy's words of wisdom.